# Andy P

## *and the gree*

Story by Maria Bird
Illustrated by Matvyn Wright

HODDER AND STOUGHTON
LONDON SYDNEY AUCKLAND TORONTO

Andy Pandy has a special box where he keeps pieces of striped cotton to mend his rompers if he tears them, ribbons for Looby Loo, and all kinds of bits and pieces to make Teddy's bows because he is always losing his.

One day he found a nice big piece of cloth, and he began to cut out an apron for Teddy, so that he could wash the cups and saucers without getting his fur all wet. Some pieces fell on the floor and Teddy picked one up. It was red with blue spots.

Then he fetched a pair of scissors and cut all round the piece of stuff, snip snap, snip snap. After that he smoothed out the red and blue piece and held it up. 'Look, Andy,' he said. 'It looks just like a duck.'

Andy Pandy was very busy sewing, but he looked up and said, 'Why, so it is! But what a funny-coloured duck. Look and see if there is a piece of yellow stuff in my special box, and then you can cut out a yellow duckling.'

Off went Teddy, and when he had found the piece of yellow woolly stuff, he sat down on the floor, and the only sound that could be heard for a long time was the snip snap of Teddy's scissors, and the soft stitch stitch of Andy's needle as he sewed Teddy's apron.

Suddenly Andy Pandy's puppy Rags rushed into the room, knocking Teddy over and scattering pieces all over the place. 'Go away, Rags,' shouted Teddy. 'You've spoiled my yellow duck. Bad dog.' Rags didn't know he was being scolded – he just wagged his tail.

Andy said, 'I expect he wants to go for a walk. We'll take him as soon as I have finished your apron.'
'Look at my duck,' said Teddy. 'He jogged my elbow and its beak is all bent, and I did want to make a yellow duck so much.'

'Never mind,' said Andy Pandy. 'When we go out, we'll go and see the ducks at the farm. We'll take some bread for them, shall we?' 'Oh yes,' said Teddy, 'and I'll save all my crusts for them at tea-time.'

RICE
RICE
BREAD

Andy smiled because Teddy was sometimes naughty about eating his crusts. He finished his sewing and Teddy was very pleased with his new apron. 'May I wear it to go to the ducks?' he asked. 'Well,' said Andy, 'it's really for washing up.'

'It's really for water,' said Teddy, 'and there's plenty of that in the duck pond.' 'Come along, then,' said Andy, and he tied the new red apron with the blue spots round what would have been Teddy's waist if he had had one. Then they set off with Rags jumping all round them.

They often went to the duck pond and every time Rags dashed in, splashing water everywhere, and the ducks pretended to be frightened and waddled up on to the bank, quacking and squawking, but really they enjoyed it as much as Rags did.

But this time when Andy and Teddy got there, they noticed that the ducks were not in the water and that the pond was covered with green weed, which was so thick that no water could be seen. Rags didn't stop to think – he just plunged into the pond.

He swam over to the other side of the pond to find out why the ducks were not swimming about as usual, and as he jumped up on to the bank, Andy Pandy and Teddy burst out laughing. Rags was quite green.

As for the ducks, they laughed so much that some of them had to lie down and wave their feet in the air. Then Rags, who didn't know what they were laughing at, shook himself, and all those beautiful white ducks were covered with green spots.

Andy and Teddy laughed more than ever at the green puppy and the spotted ducks. Then Rags shook himself again, and there was Teddy with green spots on his new apron. 'What a good thing I had it on,' he said, 'or I would have had green spots all mixed up with my fur.'

ISBN 0 340 03003 8

First published 1966
Eighth impression 1984



Published by Hodder and Stoughton Children's Books,
(a division of Hodder & Stoughton Ltd)
Mill Road, Dunton Green, Sevenoaks, Kent TN13 2YJ.

Printed in Great Britain by Adams Brothers & Shardlow Ltd, Leicester.